Enos Mills
Rocky Mountain
Naturalist

Enos Mills
Rocky Mountain Naturalist

A NOW YOU KNOW BIO

John Stansfield

Filter Press, LLC
Palmer Lake, Colorado

This work is dedicated to the spirited people who work, like Enos Mills, for the preservation of Colorado's parks, monuments, and wilderness areas: Mary King Sherman, John Otto, James Grafton Rogers, Arthur Carhart, David Brower, Howard Zahniser, Dottie Fox, Connie Harvey, Joy Caudill, Bill Mounsey, John Fielder, Mark Pearson, Steve Smith, and many others, including those in the future, who advocate for wild lands.

Library of Congress Cataloging-in-Publication Data

Stansfield, John, 1947-
  Enos Mills, Rocky Mountain naturalist / John Stansfield.
    p. cm. — (A Now you know bio)
  Includes bibliographical references (p.   ) and index.
  ISBN-13: 978-0-86541-072-5 (pbk. : alk. paper)
  1. Mills, Enos Abijah, 1870-1922—Juvenile literature. 2. Naturalists—United States—Biography—Juvenile literature. I. Title. II. Series.
  QH31.M47S73 2005
  333.72'092—dc22
                                                                    2005020272

Filter Press, LLC, P.O. Box 95, Palmer Lake, Colorado.

Printed in the United States of America

Contents

Enos Mills and a fellow climber stand silhouetted in the Keyhole rock formation on Longs Peak Trail during summer 1904. The trail passes through the Keyhole and across a boulder-strewn slope (upper right) which leads to the summit.

Introduction

Enos Mills was a sickly boy who grew into a robust, busy man. He was a naturalist, an author, a national park advocate, a public speaker, a photographer, a businessman, a mountaineer and adventurer, a miner, and a conservationist. While a young man, he bought an inn in Estes Park, Colorado. He could see the splendors of Longs Peak and the Rocky Mountains from his inn. Mills's abiding belief was that appreciation of and exposure to nature were essential to the well being of an individual and a nation. He made protection of public lands the focus of his energetic life. The creation of Rocky Mountain National Park is so identified with Mills's efforts that he is today known as "the father of Rocky Mountain National Park."

Although Mills wrote sixteen books and published hundreds of magazine and newspaper articles, he did not write an autobiography. If he had lived beyond age 52, perhaps he would have. The writer-naturalist firmly believed that all living things have their own interesting life stories. As the reader may discover in these pages, Mills was no different.

A quotation by Enos Mills opens each chapter. Beginning on page 68, the Nature of Place section provides background information on the ecology and geography of the Great Plains and Rocky Mountains. Nature activities on pages 86 – 92 provide suggestions for exploring nature based on those Mills used at his Trail School at Longs Peak Inn.

1 A Kansas Boyhood

*As a child my mother had interested me in natural
history and had fired my imagination with stories from
her own experiences among peaks and streams.
Natural history has been my "outside" interest.*

For decades during the mid-1800s, a clan made up of members of the Lamb family and Mills family migrated westward across the United States and lived close together. Many belonged to the Society of Friends, a religious group also called Quakers. The clan moved to eastern Indiana in the 1830s and on to Iowa about 1850. In the spring of 1857, newly-married Enos A. Mills, Sr. and Ann Lamb Mills migrated to Linn County, Kansas Territory. With them arrived at least 35 other family members.

"We came for the avowed purpose of helping to make Kansas a free state," Enos Mills, Sr. stated about the move to Linn County. "Here, on the border of Missouri, our trouble began. Frequent raids from Missouri border

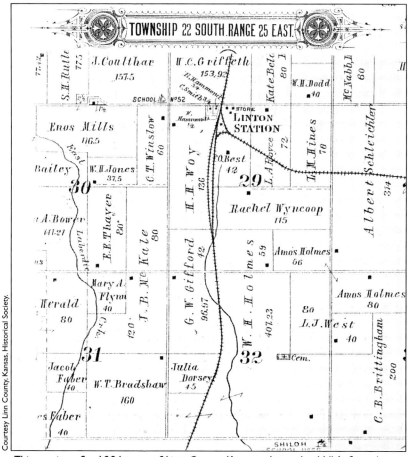

This portion of a 1906 map of Linn County, Kansas, shows the Mills's farm (upper left) and nearby the Maple Grove School, marked as School Number 52.

ruffians killed our neighbors. For seven long years we remained as a picket post."

The Battle of Mine Creek, during the American Civil War, occurred only a few miles south of the town of Pleasanton near the Mills family farm. Members of the Mills and Lamb families fought in that encounter on the side of the Union Army. The October 25, 1864 battle with Confederate cavalry was the largest on Kansas soil during the war.

Before and during the war, Mills and Lamb family members hid and transported escaped slaves, wrote letters to newspapers and Congress opposing slavery, organized

Denver Public Library, Western History Collection, #x-21803.

Beginning in 1859, "Pikes Peak or Bust" was the rallying cry of Colorado-bound emigrants, like these men photographed camping in the mountains. Enos and Ann Mills traveled toward Pikes Peak and the Rocky Mountains in 1860 in a wagon much like this one.

abolitionist meetings, and made speeches. The families did all they could to defeat the evil of human bondage. Antislavery leader Josiah Lamb, father of Ann Lamb Mills, helped draft the Kansas Constitution in 1859. The document outlawed slavery in the state. Josiah represented Linn County in the state legislature after Kansas was admitted to the United States on January 29, 1861.

Stories of gold discoveries in the Rocky Mountains inspired Ann and Enos. Like thousands of other gold-seekers, they "took the Pikes Peak fever" and headed west to the mountains by wagon in April 1860. Until Colorado Territory was created in 1861, Pikes Peak was part of Kansas Territory.

The young couple needed a change of scenery. They were mourning the deaths of their first two children. Economic times were hard. Drought choked the Kansas farms. The violence of **Bleeding Kansas** erupted often near their home. Hunting gold would give Enos and Ann a chance to sample the wonders of the Rocky Mountains.

When the couple left home, Elkanah (*El-KAY-nah*) Lamb, a double cousin of both Ann and Enos, and two other relatives went with them. All were seasoned frontier travelers. The gold-seekers followed the Platte River 500 miles across the plains to Denver.

Late in life, Enos Mills, Sr. recalled the party's travels into the mountains and across the Continental Divide: "Our course from Denver was west up the Platte river to

South Park. We stopped at the town of Tarryall in South Park and did some placer mining for a short time, and then crossed one of the ranges, where Breckenridge now stands, on Blue River. There was just one house in Breckenridge; one barrel of whiskey at 25 cents per drink. Mrs. Mills had the distinction of being the first white woman that ever crossed the range west of Tarryall."

The prospectors found little gold that summer of 1860. Wildflower carpets, evergreen forests, torrential streams, sky-reaching peaks, and strenuous outdoor adventures were the treasures they claimed. In July the family found their "gold fever" replaced by several cases of real fever, which drove them down from the mountains toward Denver.

Hearing news of famine caused by ongoing drought in eastern Kansas, the explorers chose to return to Linn County. In later years, the treasured tales of "experiences among peaks and streams" fired the imaginations of Enos and Ann's eight children, including their oldest surviving son, Enos, Jr., born April 22, 1870. The boy and his siblings longed to explore the Rockies someday as their parents had done.

Farm life meant hard work for both adults and children. Young Enos often struggled at his chores. A digestive ailment, probably an allergy to wheat, left him weak and often sick. He learned basic academic skills at

The Maple Grove School building, where Enos Mills studied through eighth grade, is used for storage today. The Mills farm, no longer owned by the family, was located in the trees in the right background.

the one-room Maple Grove School. But he showed little interest in school. Mills described himself as a dreamer in the classroom. His formal education ended with eighth grade.

What interested Enos was the natural world and its creatures. Meeting a skunk one day, Enos carefully watched as it sprayed three dogs—twice each—and two of his friends—once each—with its stinky, eye-stinging repellent. Mills approached the skunk for a closer look. "After eight performances I felt assured that of course he must be out of eradicator," Mills later wrote. "But he wasn't."

Westbound Boy

In 1884, the family doctor told Ann and Enos that their sickly son might not live if he stayed on the farm. His parents discussed sending Enos to Colorado in hopes his health might improve. If the 1860 mountain adventure fostered their recovery from stress and sorrow, might the high country help in the boy's cure? Thousands of sickly people flocked to Colorado each year for the healthful

Teenaged Enos Mills (back left) stands with sisters (left to right) Sarah, Belle, and Ella. In front from left are Enoch, Naomi, Ann Lamb Mills, Enos Mills, Sr., and Horace. The portrait was taken shortly before Enos moved to Colorado in 1884.

environment. Their cousin, Elkanah Lamb, and his family lived there now. The Lambs could watch over the boy. So, it was decided, he should go. Young Enos, learning of his journey to the mountains, must have shouted for joy when he heard the news.

He said goodbye to his family one spring morning and set out for several days travel to Kansas City, about 65 miles north. According to family accounts, the boy traveled light, mostly walking, carrying a few possessions and a little money. He spent nights with farm families along the way, working for his keep.

In Kansas City, he found work as an errand boy at a bakery. After several weeks, he had saved enough to buy a rail ticket to Denver. As Enos boarded the train, the mountains built from years of family stories loomed large in his imagination. In a matter of hours, he would see the real Rocky Mountains for himself.

2 On His Own in the Rockies

Sent West an invalid boy, I escaped most of public school and missed college. Arrived in the mountains of Colorado at the age of fourteen and in my fifteenth and sixteenth years built myself a little log cabin on the slope of Long's Peak…Landed in the West in time to know the frontier. Was intensely interested in Westerners and spent great days with the old prospector, the trapper, the capable cowboy and the Indian.

Arriving in Denver in spring 1884, young Mills did not stay long in the fast-growing city. He headed toward the mountains, the summer home of the Lamb family. At the end of the long, slow passage up a rough mountain track, a grassy valley came into view. Mills stared wide-eyed, his red hair blowing in the wind. The open valley before him, known as **Estes Park**, lay surrounded by jagged, towering peaks.

From the town of Estes Park—at that time a loose cluster of wooden buildings on the valley floor at 7,500 feet above sea level—the trail to Lamb's Ranch continued southward. Traversing eight miles of meadow and thick forest, the path rose steeply over Wind River Pass. The ranch lay in a small, open valley beyond the pass. To the southwest, the sheer face of Longs Peak soared more than 5,000 feet above the ranch cabins.

Elkanah and Jane Lamb, and their son Carlyle, welcomed the newcomer to the ranch and Longs Peak Valley (now called Tahosa Valley). Though Enos was a

Taken in 1882 by pioneering western photographer William Henry Jackson, this photograph shows a part of Estes Park (foreground). In the left background, Longs Peak (right) and Mount Meeker rise high above the park.

greenhorn, new to the West and mountain life, he was rapidly becoming a young man, growing in confidence, able to fend for himself.

Making His Own Way

Mills worked that summer of 1884 at the Elkhorn Lodge. Like many settlers in early Estes Park, the James family, owners of the Elkhorn, boarded summer travelers on their cattle ranch. In fact, they earned more money tending tourists than cattle. The Elkhorn became (and still is) a popular resort in the scenic valley. Enos chopped wood, washed dishes, fed and herded livestock, even served afternoon tea. He used skills learned on the family farm and gained new ones.

The young man migrated, as the golden eagle does, from the mountains to the prairie in fall. For three winters, he found work on farms or ranches in eastern Colorado. Like the eagle, Enos returned to the mountains in spring. These seasonal migrations set a pattern that continued for much of his life.

In 1885 the Lambs hired Enos to work for the summer at their ranch, also known as Longs Peak House. Elkanah and Carlyle Lamb served as guides for many climbing parties on Longs Peak and other mountains. Before and after their treks, climbers stayed at Longs Peak House.

The mountaineering stories heard around Longs Peak House fascinated Enos. He explored nearby trails, stopping to observe wild creatures. Carlyle taught his cousin about mountain guiding. Though still sickly at times, Mills's strength and endurance were improving with hard work, fresh air, and exercise. That summer he made his first climb of Longs Peak, helping photographers with heavy cameras to the summit at 14,259 feet above sea level.

Longs Peak, Enos discovered, commands "rugged near-by views as well as wonderful far-reaching vistas that vanish in the light and shadow of distance." He later wrote, "After one climb to the summit, I decided to become a Longs Peak guide."

The following summer at age 16, Enos climbed Longs Peak alone for the first time. He studied the trail and its surroundings, carefully planning for the time he would lead a group to the summit. The young mountaineer helped Carlyle guide parties of climbers. Together, the cousins worked with pick and shovel, making improvements to the rocky trail to ease the way for their customers. More climbers came each year to attempt the long and strenuous trek to the peak.

Mills summitted Longs Peak more than 300 times in his life. He ascended and descended on a variety of routes in all seasons and weather conditions, including lightning, hail, rain, whiteouts of snow and fog, pitch darkness,

Enos Mills (right) near the summit on his first climb of Longs Peak in 1885. The trail runs over loose, bare rock, edging around very steep cliffs.

and winds of 170 miles per hour. Of all his memorable mountaineering feats, he wrote, "the trip with Harriet was the one I like best to recall."

Harriet Peters climbed Longs Peak with Enos one late summer day, asking probing questions and making clever observations about wildlife, plants, and watersheds. At the top, she wondered about rock origins and the two discussed the effect of glaciers on the summit plateau.

Before beginning the descent, Mills stated, "(She) turned and looked silently at the far-distant, magnificent views to the north, south, east, and west. Not a question was asked and I have often wondered what impression they made on her." Harriet Peters, the perceptive naturalist, was eight years old when she summitted Longs Peak.

In 1885 American adults could file claims for government land, usually 160 acres, to establish a **homestead**. Improvements, such as constructing a building, had to be made on the land. At fifteen, Enos Mills was too young to file a homestead claim, but armed with willpower and vision, he selected land with a panoramic view lying next to the Lamb's property. A gently sloping site was leveled for building. Working mostly alone during summer and fall, the would-be homesteader cut logs to build a cabin.

The Lambs took their livestock and left for their winter home in Fort Collins as the fall of 1885 arrived. Enos stayed to work on the fourteen-by-sixteen foot cabin. He was growing used to keeping his own company.

Enos Mills (left) and Harriet Peters pose at Longs Peak's summit. At that time, the eight-year-old Arkansas girl was the youngest person known to climb the 14, 259 foot peak.

Although occasionally slowed by digestive problems, he worked hard, notching each end of the logs with an ax. Log by log, the cabin walls rose until they were higher than the young builder's head.

Heavy snow brought cabin work to a halt. Enos completed the cabin the following year and received his **homestead patent** a few years later. As a tribute to the young man's initiative and skill, the cabin stands facing Longs Peak today at the foot of the Twin Sisters Peaks on land still owned by the Mills family.

3 Nature's Big School

I had few neighbors, and so was eager to make friends with the wild birds and animals that lived near me. Often, as I stood in the doorway, looking across at Longs Peak, which towered more than five thousand feet above me, the rabbits, squirrels, and chipmunks hopped by unafraid. I moved about quietly, never harmed them, and they soon came to know that they were in a safety zone around my home.

A gusty breeze rustled the aspen leaves overhead. Beneath the trees, the teenager patiently watched the beaver pond. He studied the beaver family at work on the dam which formed the pool. Without noticing him, a coyote on the hunt skirted the water's edge, heading downstream. Later, a mule deer doe and fawn tiptoed out of the trees to get a drink.

Enos Mills spent hours, sometimes days making observations about plants and animals in the wild. Tracking bear and bighorn sheep through the first light snows of fall taught him lessons as real as those in the few treasured textbooks he possessed. Even without a teacher's guidance, Mills said, "I was always studying, by my camp-fire, in my cabin, and in Nature's big school."

When deep snow caused him to stop building his cabin in mid-October 1885, Enos stashed his tools in Lamb's barn and headed for work at a ranch on the prairie east of Denver. His goal was to learn to be a cowboy. In exchange for hard work that winter, Mills picked up a little pay, his room and board, and many new skills.

Wide Open Spaces

In late May 1886, sixteen-year-old Enos camped on the Great Plains of southeastern Wyoming before returning to the mountains. He intended "to see what wildlife lived on the prairie and how it lived," he stated in the story, "Camping On The Plains." "I felt that I was well prepared. I was certain I knew how to camp and especially that my camp equipment was correct." Enos hauled a heavy backpack across the greening grassland and set up camp near an old buffalo wallow filled with water.

Two passing cowboys, seeing all his gear, asked him if he was opening a general merchandise store. "The kid has more kitchenware than the cook at our cow camp," one said "kindly but merrily" as they rode off.

Trekking out from camp the next morning, the young naturalist observed prairie dogs barking in alarm as he approached their colony. Then he stumbled on a mother pronghorn with two young ones. Mills crept close to one of the well-camouflaged kids. He notes in the story, "not until I had touched it with my hand did it quit playing dead and rush off with the other toward the mother." Fascinated, he spent the rest of the day tracking and observing pronghorn.

When Enos tried to return to camp, he became lost. The plains, unlike the mountains, hold few large landmarks. Searching for his way until after dark, he finally made a cow chip fire, lay down on the buffalo grass, and slept.

In the morning, Mills backtracked the previous day's trail. He eventually spotted the buffalo wallow and his first campsite. Just then a **dust devil** came spinning across the prairie. The whirlwind nimbly lifted thc lighter pieces of his camp stuff, carrying them away. After the fast-moving wind storm passed, Enos "picked up fifty-seven varieties" of scattered gear. Heading toward camp with arms loaded, he came upon a burned-out campfire—his own of the night before. Mills realized then that he had spent a cold, hungry night only five hundred feet from the food and shelter of his first night's camp.

Encounters with pronghorn, prairie dog, rattlesnake, coyote, kingfisher, and other creatures made the Great Plains trek special for Mills. He reached some conclusions about camping too.

"The supreme camping test," he later wrote, "is finding the way back to camp. One who makes a mental log of his movements, who knows where he is every minute, will be able to return."

The young explorer also made decisions about what was and was not essential equipment. "From that time [on] I planned to go light. My equipment now consisted of a haversack [pack], one blanket, one waterproof canvas, a large and a small tin cup, tin pan, canteen, hatchet, pocket knife, and field glass [binoculars]. This seemed to be enough. I did not carry any kind of gun." He camped with this equipment—or even less—for hundreds of nights during the years to come.

Bachelor Father

A pair of mountain bluebirds arrived at the homestead cabin in the spring of 1886. Mills wrote in *Bird Memories of the Rockies*, "One morning before the front of the house was finished, they [bluebirds] took possession. I lived in

The feathers of the male mountain bluebird (left) scatter and reflect light to create the appearance of its bright breeding plumage.

The plain colored female bluebird (below) gathers nest-building material.

Photos by Michael Seraphin.
Courtesy Colorado Division of Wildlife

my cabin that summer without completing it, unwilling to disturb the bluebirds and the building of their nest above the ridge pole."

The male and female birds raised two **broods** of young that season. Mills studied them carefully. The parent birds grew used to him. By late summer, they trusted him enough to perch on his shoulder or writing desk. Before birds and human migrated to the Plains in October, Enos tied a copper thread around a leg of each parent. If they returned in spring, he would know.

The bluebird pair, mates for life, arrived at the completed cabin in late March 1887. They refurbished the nest above the ridgepole and raised more young, thirty-three in all during three summers. They might have returned for more summers, but in 1889 a boy, camping nearby with his family, discovered the tame birds. He shot them one day while Mills was absent. On his return, the young naturalist found five babies calling out for parents and food. "It was fortunate for me, and also for these little orphans," Mills wrote about that day, "that I had watched their mother and father feed, train, and raise a number of bluebird families." He fed the young ones worms and insects by the hundreds.

Two of the baby birds died soon after their parents were killed. The survivors lived in the cabin. They played often, with Enos and each other. He took them for walks. They followed the human closely, imprinted on him as their new parent. The birds eventually taught themselves to fly. One male—small, bright-colored, and very alert—stayed closest to Mills, watching Mills constantly. It listened carefully as he spoke and often attacked items on his desk with great joy. Enos nicknamed that bird Little Blue.

In late September, the three surviving birds joined a flock of mountain bluebirds. They headed for wintering grounds in Texas or Mexico. Soon after, Mills left Tahosa Valley for his winter's work. He returned to his cabin in July 1890. There was a nest of baby bluebirds over the ridgepole.

Leaving the door open, Enos sat down at his desk. Suddenly, he heard, "a flutter of wings, and a bird alighted on my shoulder, then on the table." The bird looked intently at Mills. "Are you Little Blue?" he asked it. "Are those your babies in the nest?" The answer to both questions was yes.

Enos Mills's cabin sits on the southwest slope of the Twin Sisters Peaks on the edge of Rocky Mountain National Park.

4 Wandering Days

I spent most of the time camping alone in the wild places without any gun…Interested in every living thing, and somewhat interested in Geology, I tried everywhere to get acquainted with the birds, the flowers and the trees…I camped and climbed much in the winter as well as in the summer and I made numerous trips by moonlight…Now and then I had to stop to earn my living. Commonly I worked in the lively mining camp of Butte, Montana, where I received big wages.

Butte, Montana, of the 1880s sat like a smoke-belching dragon in the bowl of its mountain home. Hundreds of factory stacks spewed smoke, laced with sulfur, arsenic, and other toxic chemicals. Like embers from a dying bonfire, the city glowed red in the dark. Open fire pits continuously burned mining waste.

Copper mining, **milling**, and **smelting** kept the dragon's heart rumbling loudly day and night.

The lure of five dollars a day in pay led Enos Mills from Estes Park in the fall of 1887. His strength and stamina much improved, he reportedly walked and camped most of his way to Montana. Along the way, the seventeen-year-old explorer carefully noted the birds, flowers, and trees of the Northern Rockies.

On his first day in town, the Anaconda mine hired the slim teenager as a tool boy. A tool boy was always in motion. He traveled deep underground supplying miners with sharp drills from the blacksmith aboveground. He hauled dulled tools out and began again. The day he was hired, Enos made friends with John Lloyd, also a tool boy.

Mills learned that the booming city offered more than just industry and pollution. Butte was a rich cultural stew. Thousands of people from around the world crowded the streets at all hours. Many stores, restaurants, and saloons never closed. Drunkenness, drug addiction, and gambling were common, but so were churches, good schools, and the arts. In his free time, Enos took advantage of the good things the community offered. "The city is ever ready to honor genius, reward talent or welcome merit," Mills said of Butte.

Young Enos found Butte's best educational opportunity at the free public library. As his friend John Lloyd noted, "Enos sat up half the night reading." The

Butte library became a high school and college for Mills. Enos read poetry, essays, plays, science, philosophy, economics. The library, like the world of nature, became an inspiration. "To step from a great mining camp into a library," he later wrote at age 27, "is like stepping from madness to reason; from darkness to light…Every library is a World's Fair; it contains the masterpieces of master minds."

He attended musical performances, lectures, and plays. New ideas were discussed at length with John and other friends. Mills attempted to write in various styles and joined a writer's group.

For 14 years, beginning in 1887, Enos Mills spent his winters working in the mines of Butte or other western mining boomtowns. He rose rapidly in skill and pay—tool boy, miner, machine-driller, compressor operator, night foreman, stationary engineer. A wealthy mine owner recognized the young man's initiative and aptitude. He offered Mills the chance to work year-round in mine administration. Enos turned him down. Being a mountain guide was the job he loved best and returned to almost every summer.

Mills found help with his stomach problems from a doctor in Butte, who suggested he drop starchy foods from his diet. To cleanse his system, the doctor recommended fasting for ten days and drinking only water. Enos continued to work during the fast. He felt so good at the

Miners, probably from the Anaconda Mine in Butte, Montana, pose between shifts at work in the late 1880s. Enos Mills is seated on the front bench at the far left.

end of fasting that he played in a game of baseball. On a starch-free diet, his health improved steadily.

California and an Eventful Meeting

Winters underground paid for summers outdoors on Longs Peak and around western North America. Enos lived simply, always saving what he could from his pay. Places described in books called him to travel farther afield. Mills took up what he called a "poetic" life. His was a life of exploration—a playful vagabond and daredevil pursuing the call of the wild. He sought out extreme experiences in untamed lands, tracking grizzly without a gun, descending cliff faces without ropes, outrunning forest fires, outskiing avalanches. The adventurer took serious risks and lived to tell about it.

Searing fires swept through Butte's mines in fall 1889. The damage was so extensive that many miners were put out of work for months.

Mills took advantage of the layoff and set out to see California's natural wonders. His first sighting of the ocean, rolling to the horizon like the Kansas plains, thrilled him. While walking the cliff-lined beaches of San Francisco, Enos made an unexpected discovery, one that would set the course for the rest of his life. As he tells the story, the discovery was not a plant or wild animal, but a man:

> *On the beach near the old cliff house I came upon a number of people around a small gray bearded man who had a hand full of plants which he was explaining.*
>
> *As soon as these people scattered, I asked him concerning a long-rooted plant that some one had dug from a sand dune. The man was John Muir…After giving a stirring biography of the plant [yerba buena]…he invited me for a four-mile walk across the sand hills and through Golden Gate Park…During this walk he incited me to do so many things some of which I fear will not be done by the time I reach three score and ten [years].*

In 1889, John Muir (1838-1914) was a nationally-known writer and naturalist, famous for his solo treks through California's Sierra Nevada Mountains, especially the Yosemite (Yo-SEM-it-ee) region. His efforts to preserve remarkable natural resources were rewarded in 1890, when Yosemite was designated the second national park in the United States. (Yellowstone was the first national park on earth, designated by the U. S. Congress in 1872.) Later, Muir worked to create other national parks in the West and founded the Sierra Club, a hiking and environmental protection group.

Mills later stated that the "mere chance meeting with Muir was epoch marking" for him. Muir must have recognized potential strengths in the young man. On their first walk and in later meetings and correspondence, Muir "chided, scolded, commanded and enthused" Enos to study nature carefully and constantly, to organize his thinking. He urged him to develop writing and public speaking skills. Muir told him, "I want you to help me do something for parks, forests and wildlife."

Taking Muir's advice, Mills explored the wild places of California for nearly six months. He explored the redwood and giant sequoia forests, Yosemite and western Nevada, remote ocean beaches, Death Valley, and the Mojave Desert.

Over the next decade, wanderlust—and Muir's suggestions—sent Enos traveling far away. Twice, in 1892 and 1894, he journeyed to southeast Alaska. Trekking in Yellowstone National Park alone and as part of a government survey crew filled seven months in 1891. He stated that river trips carried him down the "Missouri-Mississippi from source to sea, the Columbia, the Connecticut and the Ohio." In 1900 Mills toured Europe for a month with his uncle, Elkanah Lamb.

Famed naturalists John Burroughs (left) and John Muir relax while exploring Yosemite in 1909. Both men positively influenced Enos Mills with their writing and personal contact. Photo by Colorado photographer Fred Pay Clatworthy.

Mills began photographing scenes from his travels during the 1890s. Using a small Kodak camera, he used his photos in publications and to illustrate speeches.

Before returning to Colorado in summer 1890, Enos hiked Muir Woods with the man for whom it is named. Now a national monument, Muir Woods is a coastal redwood forest north of San Francisco. Muir was Mills's role model as outdoorsman, writer, **naturalist**, and **conservationist**.

Mills said of their relationship, "[Muir] became the factor in my life." The two remained lifelong friends.

5 Taking High Trails

For three successive winters I traversed the upper slopes
of the Rockies and explored the crest of the continent alone.
While on this work, I was instructed to make notes on
"those things that are likely to be of interest or value
to the Department of Agriculture or the Weather Bureau,"
and to be careful not to lose my life.

A voice from outside his mountain cabin startled the solitary miner. Within, he picked up his lamp and slowly opened the door. The lamplight fell on a young man with a shock of red hair, holding snow shoes in mittened hands. "May I come in and get warm?" the visitor quietly asked.

Enos Mills appeared so often in winter at the doors of isolated mountain folks that they called him the Snow

Man. Sometimes he found shelter in mining towns. Most often, after a day of rambling icy ridges and snowy valleys, Mills found himself "alone in the silence watching my campfire—watching shadows shift and dance upon the cliff."

Learning of the Snow Man and his winter treks, L. G. Carpenter, Colorado's state engineer, persuaded him to work as state snow observer. Carpenter, according to Mills, "was making some original investigations concerning forests and the water-supply." The engineer, who was also a college professor and expert in agricultural irrigation, strongly believed that ample, clean water depended on healthy forests. Mills's observations helped prove that point.

During the winters from 1902-1903 to 1904-1905, Enos Mills rambled "the wintry heights in sunshine and storm." He measured the depth and water content of snowpack at the tops of river valleys. Colorado's forests, he discovered, were being wiped away by excessive logging and fires, many caused by careless humans. In some mountain ranges, only 20 percent of original forest cover remained. Mills recorded his findings in detailed reports to Carpenter.

Winter travel in the mountains implies taking sometimes life-threatening chances. Enos carried risk-taking to new heights. He experienced falls into icy streams,

Though not always wearing a tie, Enos Mills traversed Colorado's snowy mountains for three decades, covering thousands of miles on snowshoes and skis.

unintended rides in snow slides, blizzards, subzero cold, lack of food, and frostbite. Despite living on the edge or over it, he somehow survived. The natural world seemed to give him energy. As Mills wrote, "wrestling naked-handed with the elements" was both his challenge and his joy.

The Snow Man's reputation as a mountaineer and a writer spread through Colorado and beyond. Colorado newspapers reported his adventures. To satisfy curious readers, he wrote personal stories for the *Denver Times*, the *Rocky Mountain News* and other papers. National magazines also published his articles on nature and outdoor adventure. The first appeared in *Outdoor Life* magazine in 1902.

In 1905 Mills self-published his first book, *The Story of Estes Park and a Guide Book*. Calling himself not a scholar but a guide, he stated in the foreword, "It is written because a guide book is needed, and for the purpose of conveniently recording the story of Estes Park." The guide book—rooted in the author's extensive knowledge of travel routes, accommodations, and scenic spots—met the needs of a growing number of tourists to the area. Editions of the book after 1914 omitted the guide book portion, which had become outdated. What remained, a brief, folksy history of the people who explored and settled the region, is still in print under the title, *The Story of Early Estes Park*.

After Dinner Speech

Despite having nothing to eat for two days, the snow observer struggled on through the high country. He stopped at the first cabin he saw. A neatly-dressed young woman came to the door, and he asked her for food. She blushed and then turned pale at sight of his ragtag clothing and face smeared with the charcoal he used for sunscreen. Was this an outlaw? she wondered. Behind her, children laughed. One glance told the man at the door that this was not a home. It was a one-room schoolhouse. The teacher invited him in. She and the six students shared food with the hungry mountaineer.

After dinner, Mills described his job to the small audience. He talked of the beauty and benefits of forests. He described the widespread forest destruction he had seen. The wildlife and habitats lost and streams polluted. How important the forest is for everyone and everything. In the mountain school that day, Enos Mills gave one of his first forestry speeches. It would be followed by hundreds more, presented all around the nation.

Telling Nature's Stories

In addition to his work as snow observer, Enos Mills began a career as an innkeeper in 1902. Using his savings from mining and guiding, he purchased Longs Peak House from his cousin, Carlyle Lamb. He continued the Lambs' tradition of rustic cabin comfort and hearty food, combined with the mountain guide service. Beyond these services, Mills had visions for the ranch and the region as far-reaching as the view from Longs Peak.

"For years I was a guide on Long's Peak," Enos recollected in 1917. "During this time I unconsciously evolved **Nature Guiding**—featuring Natural History on outdoor trips. My chief aim in life has been to arouse interest in the outdoors."

Mills guided on Longs Peak and other mountains until 1906. He led people to discover nature's wonders, from the massive to the miniscule. He trained both men and women as guides. In so doing, he created a new occupation, **nature interpreter**. During Mill's lifetime, women were limited to a few occupations, such as teaching, nursing, and secretarial work. Mills believed in the equality of the sexes and advocated for women in outdoor careers.

Today, interpreters work worldwide in thousands of parks, forests, nature centers, museums, and on cruise ships. The National Park Service's interpretive programs are built on a foundation established by Enos Mills. Interpreters know, as he did, that "nature's storybook is everywhere and always open." They know that by hearing these stories, the "biographies" of plants, animals, and natural processes, listeners more deeply understand and value their world.

Keeping the Inn

When Mills bought Longs Peak House, it accommodated twenty guests in the main lodge and scattered cabins. He renamed it Longs Peak Inn in 1904. Rates for room and board ranged from $2.50 to $4.00 per day. Under his direction, the inn grew to serve 100 guests at a time with 35 employees during the summer season.

On June 4, 1906, while Enos was speaking at a convention in St. Paul, Minnesota, the main lodge burned to the ground. He immediately borrowed money to rebuild the inn. He designed a larger replacement in harmony with the surrounding forest. A master carpenter built the new inn of fire-killed, weather-sculpted trees salvaged from slopes nearby. "The finished structure was a good combination of the rustic and the artistic. We 'builded' far wiser than we knew," Mills wrote in *Sunset* magazine. Guests enjoyed the first meal in the new dining room on the Fourth of July.

In a 1911 article about the inn from *The Craftsman* magazine, writer M. Kennedy Bailey stated that the buildings showed "[Mills's] own respect for nature's handiwork." This was also true of the attitude the place

Enos Mills wanted his guests at Longs Peak Inn (above) to be close to nature indoors as well as outdoors. Longs Peak dominates in the background of the photograph.

The inn's stairway (right), crafted of weathered logs, drew visitors to its natural detail.

At Longs Peak Inn
>You will hear the

Call of the Wild

Nature will be your neighbor.

Higher than any hotel in the Alps.

Above troubleline and near timberline and snow.

The place to meet Long's Peak
>and see the Rockies.

TRAILS to the silent places

and the heights.

Evergreens and their rich aroma.

No consumptives taken.

The house stands by a mountain
>brook in a wild flower garden.

Fringed blue gentians and columbines.

Comfort and home flavored meals.

Pine knots blaze in the big fireplace.

>– Enos A. Mills

Estes Park   **Colorado**

This advertisement for Longs Peak Inn was included in the 1905 first edition of Enos Mills's The Story of Estes Park and a Guide Book.

brought out in its visitors. Guests spent active days on foot or horseback exploring peaks and glaciers, streams, and forests. They passed peaceful evenings in discussions with Mills, inspecting the Nature Room's field guides and nature specimens, moonlight hiking, or admiring the sunset on Twin Sisters ridge. Dances, bands, card-playing, and alcohol were prohibited.

The Inn's setting and its owner kept guests focused on the natural gifts of the Longs Peak region. Nellie Stevenson, a college-age visitor in 1907, described it in a letter as, "The most beautiful spot in God's whole garden."

Young visitors learned from the informal nature discovery walks of the inn's Trail School. "The school—the great outdoors—is in session whenever children wander over the trail, free from academic **chaperonage**," Mills claimed. "The trail supplies materials and equipment, and Mother Nature is an endless mental stimulus."

Two orphaned grizzly bear cubs named Johnny and Jenny helped build Longs Peak Inn's reputation for being close to nature.

Mills captured the cubs in 1903 to study their behavior and gauge their intelligence. They fascinated the summer guests. By the fall, the bears had grown so large that he sent them to the Denver zoo, where they lived out the rest of their long lives.

Faithful Scotch

A friend gave Mills a gift in 1902. It was a border collie pup named Scotch. "Of this little rustic Inn," one frequent guest wrote, "Scotch was no less the host than his master. He welcomed the coming and sped the parting guest…He stood between the coyotes and the inhabitants of the chicken yard. He was always ready to play football for the entertainment of the guests after dinner. He was really the busiest person about the Inn from morning till night." The clever collie accompanied the Colorado snow observer on many of his hazardous winter expeditions.

Scotch once saved the life of a strong-willed solo climber he accompanied on Longs Peak. The climber arrived at the summit late in the day and lost the trail down in the dark. She would not let Scotch lead her back to the trail. The dog huddled close to the young woman, keeping her alive through a freezing night. One of the Inn's nature guides discovered the guest at dawn and helped her down the mountain. His job done, Scotch hurried home for breakfast.

Mills credited Scotch with another daring rescue. One autumn day, a forest fire roared toward the dog and his injured master, who took shelter on a rocky crag above the advancing flames. On command, Scotch took Mills's jacket in his mouth and raced through the flames to a

Mills pets Scotch on the porch of Longs Peak Inn. Enos shared the dog's eventful life in his book, The Story of Scotch.

creek below for water. Scotch returned with the wet coat, his hair and skin burned. Mills wrapped himself and the dog inside the wet coat. "Flames surged around, but at last swept over and left us both alive. Without the help of Scotch, I must have perished," Mills wrote in his popular book, *The Story of Scotch.*

Scotch often helped Mills put out fires. This skill was his undoing. The collie tried to extinguish a lit dynamite fuse at a highway project site near the inn in 1910. The explosion killed him instantly. Newspapers in Denver, Chicago, and other cities reported Scotch's death. Notes of regret and remembrance arrived from all over the country. Mills never kept another dog at Longs Peak Inn.

6 A Voice for Forests and Parks

[John Muir] insisted that I must learn to write and speak…For a time I was the special agent of the Government and allowed to make Forestry addresses anywhere in the United States that opportunity afforded or that I chose.

Before radio, television, and the Internet, public speaking and writing for publications offered the best ways to reach the public. John Muir impacted millions with his artful writing, but the shy champion of wilderness areas disliked public speaking. The outgoing Enos Mills, however, far surpassed his mentor in front of audiences.

Inspired by Muir, Enos said he attempted to give a forestry talk in San Francisco at age 21, but stumbled in the effort. His first successful public address took place in Kansas City in 1895. The following year, a teachers' convention in his birthplace of Linn County, Kansas, heard him speak on the Inca people of Peru. They listened with "rapt attention," according to a local newspaper. Mills was paid $25 for the speech. He delivered Estes Park's Independence Day address on July 4, 1897. On his way to Europe in spring 1900, he spoke to audiences in Chicago and New York. As his skill and reputation grew, invitations to speak came from around the country.

His standard speech was titled "Our Greatest Friend and Most Valuable Resource—The Forest." The talk cleverly mixed statistics with sentiment, short personal stories with challenging ideas, and many conservation messages with a few appeals for the preservation of special forested places. The speaker used projected slides of his photographs to illustrate some of the talks. An Omaha newspaper in 1907 reported that Mills spoke out for the practical benefits of trees as "fully and convincingly (as) he did their esthetic value."

The forest speech changed to fit the audience and location. In Colorado, he highlighted restoring forests to protect healthy watersheds. In Waco, Texas, his presentation focused on the relationship between birds and forests. In Appalachia, the speech focused on a hot local issue, the creation of federal forest reserves (now called national forests). Some messages remained unchanged everywhere. "No country has ever grown poor by maintaining a forest" and "Evergreens are beautiful" were consistent themes.

When Longs Peak Inn closed for the season in fall 1905, Mills set off on his first extended **lecture tour**. In the eastern United States, he gave more than sixty speeches and rarely charged for them. "I talk forestry everywhere I can," he told a newspaper reporter. "I have talked in grammar schools, in colleges, in preparatory schools, before women's clubs, and in men's congresses."

Courtesy Denver Public Library, Western History Department, f-47174.

As forestry lecturer for the U. S. government, Enos Mills, seen here about 1908, traveled thousands of miles, mostly by train, during two and one-half years on the lecture circuit.

When asked why, he replied, "I want to save the forests…This is my life. It is pure joy."

His western speaking trip in early 1906 ended in June at the national convention of the General Federation of Women's Clubs in St. Paul, Minnesota. Enos energized the large audience with his conservation message. The *St. Paul Daily Dispatch* reported, "Mr. Mills has been the particular hit of the Convention." He was flooded with requests to speak to women's clubs all around the country. On June 4, the day of his speech, Mills received a telegram stating, "Long's Peak Inn burned to the ground." A house fire, not a forest fire, was the cause. With the tourist season just beginning, Mills's livelihood was at risk. He hurried to Colorado to rebuild the inn.

By fall, the lecturer was back on the road for more than fifty engagements, starting in Colorado and ending in Boston. On this tour, Mills was paid for some speeches. He usually traveled by railroad, the fastest transportation in his time. He stayed with host families or in hotels, but when he could, he camped out. Eventually, Enos claimed to have slept "by a camp-fire alone and unarmed in every state in the Union and also in Mexico, Canada, and Alaska."

As he crisscrossed the country, Mills worked on tour details, letters, and articles. The stories appeared frequently in national magazines for adults and young people. Travel gave him the opportunity to meet editors and publishers and make influential friends. In New York, he swapped stories with the famous naturalist John Burroughs. The governor of Georgia heard Enos tell "The Story of a Thousand Year Pine," an eloquent nature story. He was so moved that he brought Mills home after the speech to retell it for his wife and daughter.

Special Agent

President Theodore Roosevelt, an avid conservationist, found in Mills a perfect spokesman for forest conservation. In January 1907, Roosevelt created for him the position of government lecturer on forestry, working under Gifford Pinchot, head of the new U. S. Forest Service. Mills was paid $2,400 a year plus expenses to continue educating people about forests.

For two and one-half years, Mills traveled in fall, winter, and spring, speaking to hundreds of thousands of children and adults. During one seven-month period, he delivered more than 125 lectures in 36 different states. Mills and other forest advocates helped convince Americans and their elected officials that the best future for the nation lay in the conservation and preservation of public lands—not in the despoiling and disposing of them. Through their effective public relations efforts the fledgling national forest program took flight.

LECTURE

To-Night

AT

Carnegie Hall

February 22nd, at 8 o'clock p. m.

ON

"Our Friends, The Trees"

BY

HON. ENOS A MILLS

OF COLORADO.

This address will be on the subject of "Forestry" and by one who is an official of the United States Agricultural Department in Washington. Mr. Mills is an able speaker and master of his subject.

Admission Free

UNION LABEL Courier and Times Press.

A poster advertising a lecture by Mills.

The Government Lecturer on Forestry resigned in May 1909. His time and abundant energy were required for other tasks. Another busy summer of innkeeping awaited him. Beyond that, Mills envisioned a campaign more challenging than any mountaineering feat: the preservation of scenery visible from his own doorstep.

The Estes Park Project

The year 1909 was a landmark for Enos Mills. Many Americans recognized his name and knew that he stood for a healthy natural world. That year, his book, *Wild Life on the Rockies*, was published and distributed nationwide. Twenty-four of the author's original photos were included. The book won praise from reviewers. The *Philadelphia Press* stated, "Extraordinary interest attaches to his narratives of exciting adventure with snowslides, wild beasts, and wild weather [in] the Rockies." In the fall, Mills launched what he, at first, called "the Estes Park project," his personal, six-year crusade for the creation of Rocky Mountain National Park.

Visitors from across America and other countries praised the scenery, natural values, and recreation offered by the Estes Park region. They likened the mountains to the Alps of Europe. The ever-growing tourist trade of the early 1900s surpassed the region's ranching, timbering, and mining businesses in economic value. Outdoor recreation, restoration of wild animal populations decimated by uncontrolled hunting and fishing, and protection of wildlife habitats became important goals for many local residents. Their foremost objective was the "conservation of scenery," protecting natural landscapes from destructive development, which Mills wrote about in his book, *The Rocky Mountain Wonderland*.

During the first decade of the twentieth century, local residents and businesspeople, Enos Mills among them, held discussions about projects to benefit the community and surrounding environment. The talks led to the formation in 1906 of the Estes Park Protective and Improvement Association (EPPIA).

In 1907 Forest Supervisor Herbert N. Wheeler proposed to EPPIA a thousand square mile "game refuge" within the Medicine Bow National Forest which surrounded the town of Estes Park. Wheeler recognized the need to restore wildlife populations decimated by over-hunting and to foster the region's growing recreational popularity. He also knew that national park lands would be removed from his administration, cutting the heart out of the newly created national forest. In September 1909 EPPIA members unanimously endorsed seeking government designation for the wildlife refuge.

Mills, however, published his own plan for an Estes National Park that September. It stated, in part, that local sites were "already extensively used as places of recreation. If they are to be permanently and more extensively used and preserved it will be necessary to hold them as public property and protect them within a national park." The suggested size of the park project was the same as Wheeler's proposed refuge, about 645,000 acres. EPPIA endorsed the national park concept.

Enos Mills had long lectured and written on the need for national forests. But for protection of his own 'big back yard', he believed that a national park was the only choice. Even though there was yet no federal management agency for parks, he favored the park alternative. The U. S. Forest Service was created in 1905 to oversee the commercial sale of trees, forage, and other resources. Scenic preservation was not then a forest service goal.

National park advocates, including Mills, mistrusted the new agency's **wise-use** conservation approach. As time went on, he suspected Forest Service staff in Colorado and Washington, D.C., of sabotaging the Estes National Park effort. Conflicts over cattle grazing on forest lands near Longs Peak Inn added fuel to the fire. With the aggressiveness of a guard dog, Mills attacked the forest service in letters and speeches. Associates tried to persuade him to tone down his attacks. Their pleas for personal restraint and political compromise mostly went unheeded.

As with mountaineering and innkeeping, Mills approached the Estes Park project boldly and energetically.

His powerful speeches on the lecture circuit won many converts to the idea of a national park. From 1909 to 1915, he addressed an estimated 300 audiences in Colorado and throughout the nation. Enos labored over hundreds of letters and articles as well. "This campaigning annihilates me and on arrival home I felt so aged," he wrote fellow park supporter J. Horace McFarland, of the American Civic Association, after a five-month speaking tour in 1911 and 1912. Enos lobbied in Washington and testified twice before Congress. In public, he never expressed any doubt that the national park would soon be a reality.

7 Triumph and Trial

*The seven-year campaign for the creation of Rocky
Mountain National Park and then the establishment of
a National Park Service was the most strenuous and
growth-compelling occupation that I have ever followed.
I am now endeavoring to have all parks managed
by themselves for their higher values. Park management
cannot be combined with management of things
commercial and be a success.*

The Estes Park project received a boost in January
1913 when a federal report called the park idea
"highly desirable," recommending a preserve
of 700 square miles. The report used the name "Rocky
Mountain National Park" for the first time. The
next month, Colorado Congressman Edward Taylor
introduced legislation to create the park. Many national
organizations supported the measure, including John

Muir's Sierra Club. "I'm heartily with you in your plan for a National Park in Colorado," Muir wrote Mills in 1910.

Colorado park supporters included EPPIA, the Colorado legislature, many business and civic groups, major newspapers, and a hiking and conservation group inspired by Mills, the Colorado Mountain Club, organized in 1912. The club's president, lawyer James Grafton Rogers, drafted and later reworked the Rocky Mountain National Park legislation.

Rogers and Mills led the effort in Colorado, though they sometimes argued over strategy. Mills hated compromise, but Rogers knew the political process often demanded it. At the outset, Mills believed Rogers gave away too much. The language of the draft park bill in February 1913 allowed grazing, mining, and timbering. This greatly alarmed Mills, who was always suspicious of Forest Service "conniving." Even the chief of the Forest Service objected to the bill, stating "[It] makes the policies of use and development…[of] the National Forests applicable to National Parks."

Mills's quick temper and determined individualism made it hard for him to be a team player. After a disagreement in 1914, Rogers warned Denver park supporters that Mills "can do those who hope for the park…considerable harm if his feelings are hurt." Several times Rogers publically downplayed Mills's importance in the park campaign. In truth, the men brought differing, but essential skills to the effort.

Building public consensus and changing government policy take an agonizing amount of time. Despite supporters' wish for speed, the park legislation plodded slowly through Congress, like a tired hiker nearing the end of the trail. Legislators spent nearly two year deliberating and revising the measure.

Among park bill opponents was a small group of Tahosa Valley residents known as the Front Range Settlers' League. Many of them were neighbors of Enos Mills. Sadly, the list of opponents also included his elderly relatives and foster parents, Elkanah and Jane Lamb. In a 1911 flyer, the League claimed that "park promoters" threatened their "homes, interests, and local autonomy." Mills was surely one of the promoters denounced by the flyer. He clearly had made enemies of former friends. A league member blamed the turnabout on Enos's "inexplicable change of character since his absurd egotism led him astray." In other words, he believed that national fame had given the park advocate a big head.

In the end, overwhelming public support for the park won out. On January 26, 1915, President Woodrow Wilson signed the act creating Rocky Mountain National Park. The thirteenth U. S. national park encompassed 359 square miles. Though expanded to about 417 square miles

Enos Mills (upper left) served as master of ceremonies for the dedication of Rocky Mountain National Park on September 4, 1915. He called it the "proudest moment of his life."

(267,000 acres) today, it is less than half the size Mills first proposed.

The *Denver Post* and other newspapers hailed Enos Mills as "the father" of the new park, a term he later used for himself. In reality, the glory never belonged to him alone. Many men and women played important, if less visible, roles in the park's estabishement. Perhaps "ramrod", "promoter", or "ardent advocate" are as suitable terms as "father" for Mills. Through his intense and sustained efforts, he earned them all.

Years and miles of wilderness walking build stamina in a body and a mind. During the "strenuous and growth-compelling" time of the park campaign and beyond, Enos lived life at a racer's pace. Longs Peak Inn, expanded in 1916, continued to enjoy a brisk summer business. Books, long and short, took form at the writer's desk in his cabin. These included *The Spell of the Rockies* (1911), *In Beaver World* (1913), *The Story of a Thousand Year Pine* (1914), *The Rocky Mountain Wonderland* (1915), and *The Story of Scotch* (1916).

The National Park Service

During the push for the establishment of Rocky Mountain National Park, advocates also lobbied for one agency to oversee the growing number of parks. "The trouble is that the National Parks, properly speaking, have not been managed at all," Mills wrote, "Each has been

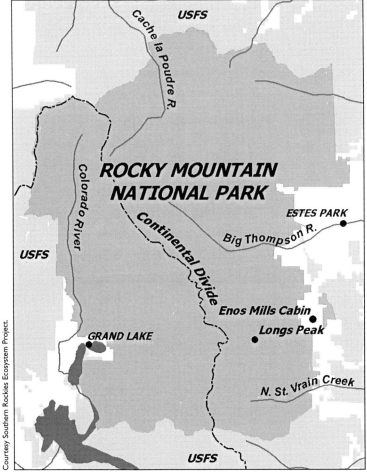

A contemporary map of Rocky Mountain National Park shows designated wilderness areas on U. S. Forest Service (USFS) lands to the north, west, and south adjacent to the park.

treated as a separate thing." Park supporters nationwide stressed the on-going economic, recreational, and spiritual benefits of a well-run, well-funded park system financed and managed by the federal government.

The creation of the National Park Service by Congress in August 1916 solved the management problem. The new agency was charged with balancing public use with the preservation of natural and historic resources in order to "leave them unimpaired for the enjoyment of future generations." This balancing act has always been a difficult task for the Park Service.

Your National Parks, Mills's detailed guide to present and proposed parks in North America, was published early in 1917. The book updated John Muir's *Our National Parks* (1901) and contained a chapter honoring him. Muir had lobbied hard for the creation of the Park Service, but he died in December 1914, before seeing it happen.

The new agency held a National Park Conference in Washington in January 1917. Enos directed a session on recreation use in parks, presented an evening of bear stories, and addressed the attendees on the topic, "National Parks for All the People." He spoke positively for the role of women in running and interpreting the parks. He spoke against granting **concessions,** arguing that businesses should not be given exclusive rights to provide services within a park.

No Concession on Concessions

In *Your National Parks*, Enos Mills stated, "Concessions are a bad feature in any park." He did not oppose businesses, such as his own Longs Peak Inn, benefiting from a nearby park. Boosting local economies was a prime reason he favored parks. However, to Mills a concession was a monopoly, limiting visitors' freedom of access to public lands and roads. He found an example close by. A transportation concessionaire conducted tours for visitors on public roads through the taxpayer-supported Rocky Mountain National Park, while other businesses, like the Inn, were banned from doing so.

Stephen Mather, then director of the park service, believed concessions promoted park visitation and the development of park facilities. Enos claimed that Mather was "farming these parks out to monopolies…over which the public have no control." As was the case with the Forest Service, Mills went, in a short time, from warm friend to bitter enemy of the park agency he helped create.

To prove his point about the 1919 transportation concession, Mills sent a car with guests from Longs Peak Inn into Rocky Mountain National Park. Park service rangers turned it back. The innkeeper sued the park service, claiming the concession policy was illegal. Legal wrangling with the Park Service continued for years. As in previous conflicts, he lectured and wrote extensively on the concession issue. But unlike the forest and park campaigns, Enos did not see this one to a successful end.

Family and Final Days

Enos often greeted inn guests with the question, "Glad you're living?" Despite many struggles, he had much to be glad about as he approached age fifty. Though never very profitable, Longs Peak Inn was a success, offering thousands a pathway to deeper understanding of nature and the peace it provides. Just beyond the inn, the new national park ensured the permanent preservation of a remarkable landscape. Reviewers praised the writer's latest books, *The Grizzly: Our Greatest Wild Animal* (1919) and *Adventures of a Nature Guide* (1920). And, after decades on his own, he found a wife.

Esther Burnell, a twenty-seven-year-old interior decorator from Cleveland, came to the inn in 1916 seeking relief from her stressful job. Enchanted by the natural beauty of the park, she stayed. Burnell roamed the trails, observing wildlife and searching outside the park for land to homestead. She worked part-time for Mills as his secretary. She homesteaded land west of the town of Estes Park and designed and oversaw building of her cabin. In the summer of 1917, she worked for Mills as a nature guide. Esther and Enos shared many interests and grew

Enos Mills visits his homestead cabin with daughter Enda. Twin Sisters Peaks (upper right) rise above them.

close. They married in August 1918. Their only child, Enda, was born April 27, 1919. "We have a red-headed baby girl at our home!" Mills wrote friends.

The vigor of Enos Mills's life slipped away and faded as quickly as the light of a mountain sunset. A variety of ills and mishaps sped his decline. He suffered broken ribs and possibly a punctured lung in a subway accident in January 1922, while in New York campaigning against concessions. A severe case of flu set in soon after he returned home. Abscessed teeth poisoned his body that summer.

And, on the morning of September 22, 1922, he suffered a fatal heart attack. Enos Mills was 52.

At Mills's request, his funeral was simple. No eulogy was offered. A friend read to 300 attendees from works of Muir, John Burroughs, Alfred Lord Tennyson, and Mills himself. Under stormy skies, six pallbearers carried the casket uphill from the inn to a grave site next to his homestead cabin. Emerson Lynn, the inn manager, remarked on "the beautiful sunset that did fill the western sky just as the body was lowered into the grave."

Mills's body rested in this grave for a short while until his wife had his body disinterred and cremated. His ashes were spread in his beloved mountains.

Courtesy Colorado Historical Society, 86-296-3170.

Newspapers and magazines nationwide offered tribute to the man and his deeds. The headline in the *Denver Express* stated, "A Big Man Lies Dead At Longs Peak." Letters of condolence to Mrs. Mills poured in from friends and strangers whose lives had been touched by her husband.

"It is as if a mountain peak has sunk below the horizon," wrote English novelist Thomas Hardy.

Enos Mills possessed equal parts of strength, intelligence, and determination. From boyhood on, his bond with mountains and wilderness inspired him to overcome serious illness and the lack of formal education, money, or influential family. Wilderness adventurer, homesteader, miner, keen observer and interpreter of nature, inspiring speaker, photographer, successful businessman, environmental pioneer—all these titles fit him well. As boy and as man, he lived a remarkable mountain life.

The legacy of Enos Mills lives on in the national park system, his books, the occupation of nature interpreter, and the homestead cabin in Tahosa Valley which his decendants maintain as a museum. Mills's foremost legacy is found in his words at the 1915 dedication of Rocky Mountain National Park. "In years to come when I am asleep forever beneath the pines, thousands of families will find rest and hope in this park, and on through the years others will come and be happy in the splendid scenes that I helped to save for them."

The Nature of Place

Enos Mills spent most of his life exploring and observing nature, especially in the American West. He educated others about the natural heritage and cultural histories of its diverse landscapes. This chapter, **The Nature of Place,** provides brief geographic, ecological, and historic information about the lands that played an important role in Mills's life. There are seven **Nature of Place** sections, one for each chapter.

1 A Kansas Boyhood
Linn County, Kansas

As a boy, Enos Mills wandered the rolling hills, prairies, and wooded hollows of home in Linn County, Kansas. The county, located in east central Kansas on the Missouri border, is part of the geographic region known as the Osage Plains. This diverse landscape receives more precipitation, averaging better than 35 inches per year, than the Great Plains farther west. Cold winters alternate with hot summers in a cycle of four distinct seasons.

In unplowed portions of the native tallgrass prairie, big bluestem grass stands taller than a boy's head. Shallow valleys, filled with pin oak, pecan, and sycamore trees, border the grassy openings. White-tailed deer, coyotes, woodchucks, and raccoons quietly seek out food beneath broad-reaching limbs. In spring, mating birds fill the woods with varied song. Meandering creeks flow to a slow river called the *Marais des Cygnes*, a French name meaning the Marsh of Swans. Ducks, geese, and wading birds nest at the dark water's edge.

Native Americans, including the Osage and Kansa tribes, have found food in the region's fertile lands and waters for thousands of years. Since the 1850s, farm families have grown crops and raised livestock on the Osage Plains. Today, much of the area economy still comes from agriculture. One of the earliest settlements in

Kansas, Trading Post, is located in Linn County on the banks of the Marais des Cygnes.

In 1854, the U. S. Congress created Kansas Territory, without deciding an important question. Would slavery be legal in Kansas? Many abolitionist emigrants rushed to settle in eastern Kansas, hoping to keep the territory and future state free of slavery. Slavery supporters, from nearby Missouri and other southern states, violently disagreed. They attacked homesteads and villages settled by "Free-Staters." Radical abolitionist John Brown, his sons, and other militants executed raids on pro-slavery settlers. From 1854 to the onset of the American Civil War in 1861, life proved turbulent and often dangerous in what was then called Bleeding Kansas.

Learn more about John Brown and the pre-Civil War era in history books and websites.

2 On His Own in the Rockies
The Great Plains

Riding west on the train at age 14, Enos Mills saw his field of view change from close-in pasture and forest to open space extending to the far horizon. The mix of sheltering woodlands and open prairies he knew disappeared soon after departing Kansas City. Trees retreated into narrow belts along streams twisting through shallow valleys. Drought-resistant grasses stretched out across the rolling land of the Flint Hills and Smoky Hills. Towns were smaller and fewer. Families lived farther apart. Like a thin jacket, shortgrass prairie covered the massive table lands of western Kansas and eastern Colorado.

The geographical term *Great Plains* describes the level, dry, mostly treeless region of the United States and Canada east of the Rocky Mountains. Though often used interchangeably with Great Plains, the words *prairie* and *grassland,* are biological terms referring to plant **communities** made up mainly of grasses. **Prairie** and **grassland** communities are found in many parts of the world, not just the middle of North America.

Though they sometimes appear barren, the grasslands provide homes to a great variety of animals. Prairie plants provide nutritious food for grass eaters. An estimated sixty million wild bison once grazed the Great Plains. Thousands of pronghorn (sometimes called antelope) still

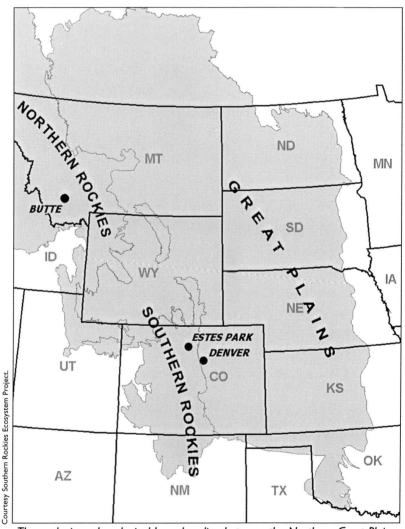

The geologic and ecological boundary line between the Northern Great Plains and the Northern and Southern Rocky Mountains, depicted in this map, winds across the heart of the continent for thousands of miles.

The Great Plains sit in a "rain shadow" created by the Rocky Mountains. The high western slopes of the mountains catch eastbound weather systems, causing rain and snow to fall on their slopes. Little moisture remains for the storms to drop on the lands farther east in the mountain shadow. The Great Plains extend almost 600 miles between Kansas City and Denver. Drought-tolerant grassland communities blanket much of Kansas and the eastern one-third of Colorado. The region receives only 12 to 20 inches of precipitation a year. Review maps of Kansas and Colorado to see how lack of precipitation affects the distribution of human population.

do. More than sixty different species of animals live in and around prairie dog towns. Colonies of these burrowing ground squirrels stretched for miles in the time of Enos Mills. Today, plowing for crops and urban development have taken a toll on the animals. Intentional poisoning also reduces prairie dog populations and impacts species that depend on the colonies, such as swift fox, black-footed ferret, and burrowing owl.

3 Nature's Big School
The Southern Rocky Mountains

Viewed from the plains about 50 miles east of Denver, the Rocky Mountains appear above the prairie like the tops of a white picket fence. Just west of the Mile High City, the geography shifts rapidly. The earth's crust wrinkles like crumpling paper. Prairie ecosystems end and mountain communities of life begin. What appeared as a picket fence from afar, now rises as a ragged stone-topped rampart more than a mile and a half high.

Plant communities change with the Rockies rise in elevation. Seen from a distance, bands of varied color sweep horizontally across the mountain faces, like earth-tone stripes in a waving flag. These color bands are made up of differing types of trees and other plants. Lighter-colored grasses, bushes, and scattered trees inhabit the

The Rocky Mountains make up about half of the land mass of Colorado, the nation's highest state. Many great rivers begin in Colorado's mountains. The Arkansas, Colorado, Rio Grande, and Platte—all grow from melting mountain snow packs, providing water to much of the American Midwest and Southwest. Tahosa Creek, flowing by Enos Mills cabin, feeds the Platte River. Using maps, follow Tahosa Creek's water as it flows to the Gulf of Mexico.

drier Foothills zone. At wetter, higher elevations, in the **montane** and **subalpine** regions, darker forests and meadows flourish. On the highest peaks, wind, cold, and

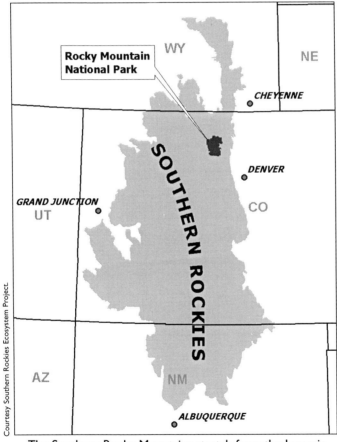

The Southern Rocky Mountains stretch from the Laramie Range in Wyoming to the Sangre de Cristo Mountains in northern New Mexico. This region has on average the highest elevation in the United States.

short growing season stop forest growth at what scientists call the **tree limit**, the highest elevation at which trees can grow.

On the highest mountain ranges, low shrubs, grasses, and other flowering plants cling to thin, rocky soil. This is the **alpine** zone, the land above the trees. Its plant community, called alpine **tundra**, is either covered with snow much of the year or exposed to intense wind, sun, and cold. These factors constantly challenge the survival of tundra plants, whose growing season lasts only a few weeks.

Mountain environments support an array of remarkable animals. Some, like the pika, live year-round in the high mountains. Bighorn sheep flourish from the foothills to the alpine zone. Other creatures, including birds and humans, migrate between plains and mountains depending on the season.

4 Wandering Days
Longs Peak

With 1.3 billion-year-old granite walls deeply sculpted by glaciers, Longs Peak is a climber's magnet. Though difficult and sometimes dangerous, the climb delivers head-spinning, 360-degree views from the slopes and summit of the peak. Wild creatures roam the mountain's shoulders, seeking a habitat that will sustain life.

When Enos Mills explored the Rockies, he often observed predator animals on the hunt. Since his time, two of the largest predators, grey wolf and grizzly bear, have been hunted to extinction in the Southern Rockies. Mountain lion, coyote, pine marten, and other carnivores prey on smaller animals. This leaves large animals, like wapiti (WA-pit-ee), also known as elk, with few predators, except humans. Lack of large predators is a major reason for overpopulation and disease among wapiti in the Longs Peak region today.

Who was the first human to view the world from the sky island of Longs Peak's summit? American Indian stories say that Gun, an Arapahoe hunting eagles, may have been the first human to the top. Major John Wesley Powell, geographer and Colorado River explorer, led the first recorded successful climb in 1868. Addie Alexander from St. Louis was the first woman known to summit Longs Peak in 1871. Most certainly, Enos Mills holds the record for most ascents, with over 300. From 1885 to 1906, Enos led 257 climbing parties to the top. In the thirty-one days of August 1906, his last year as a guide, he made thirty-two Peak trips, including six by moonlight. Today, thousands each year follow the routes of early mountaineers. Other climbers pioneer new routes to the top with ropes and rock climbing equipment.

The Longs Peak Trail leads a hiker through two communities of life: subalpine and alpine. It begins near 9,500 feet elevation on the mountain's east side in the subalpine. The path winds upward through a dense stand of lodgepole pine. Seed-collecting chickaree squirrels bark at passing hikers. Dipper birds, also called water ouzels, dive for insects in nearby Alpine Brook, its banks lined with fragrant wildflowers in summer. The trail traverses cool groves of spruce. At 10,500 feet, open ground and low willow thickets appear. Evidence of past forest fires and new tree growth mark surrounding slopes. Bushy limber pines squat on sunny, wind-blasted ridges above the trail.

Above 11,000 feet elevation on the trail, fingers of forest reach up the mountain. Stunted and shaped by fierce winds, they form the tree limit. The alpine community begins here. Tundra plants extend out from the trail's edge like a carpet. Above 12,000 foot Granite Pass, vegetation retreats into sheltered niches. The steepening trail continues on often unstable bare rock to the summit 14,259 feet above sea level. Longs Peak has the fifteenth highest summit in Colorado. Find Longs Peak and the mountains with higher summits on a Colorado map.

5 Taking High Trails
Rocky Mountain Winter

The Rocky Mountains form a gigantic, weather-catching wall. Moist weather systems, born in the Pacific Ocean, move eastward across North America. Mountains force the systems, called low air masses, upward. Water vapor in each air mass cools as it rises, forming clouds over the mountains. Depending on the temperature, rain or snow falls out on the slopes. Cold conditions in the high Rockies create snow in fall, winter, spring, and sometimes in summer.

Mountain snow means life to plants and animals in many ways. A white blanket insulates plants from winter's intense cold and wind. Mice, pocket gophers, and other small rodents find food and protection by tunneling and nesting where snow meets ground. Weasels, their fur turned white for winter camouflage, hunt the tunnels for rodent prey. The coats of snowshoe hare and ptarmigan birds take on white coloration for protection from predators. Wading through snow, long-legged moose nibble on willows.

Mountain weather can take life, as well as give it. Storms bring intense winds, subzero temperatures, snow and ice. Human fingers, toes, ears, and noses are lost to frostbite. Trapped by blizzards, people and other animals sometimes starve. Wind blows snow onto steep slopes.

When conditions are right, avalanches sweep downhill, smashing trees, large and small, and any other living things in their path. Enos Mills understood the dangers of mountain weather, saying, "sometimes with storm or snowslide [life] is in deadly earnest."

Rivers of melting snow benefit people and other creatures. It makes streams sing, forests grow, and mountain meadows bloom. It spins turbines to generate electricity. It quenches thirsts. It gives fish a home. For centuries, people around the world have used mountain water to irrigate their crops. Enos Mills helped in Colorado's first attempts to scientifically study snow and calculate snowmelt runoff. Investigate the system that brings water to your home. Where does the water you use come from?

6 A Voice for Forests and Parks
The Public Lands

Beginning in 1785, the U. S. government surveyed and mapped its undeveloped lands. At first, the only goal was to sell parcels of land at low prices to encourage the country's growth. As people moved west, they claimed land for homesteading, farming, timbering, mining, and building towns. Congress provided large land grants as financial incentives to western railroads. For their own profit, some land speculators found ways to cheat homesteaders or the government out of land and natural resources.

By the 1870s, excessive logging, overgrazing, and destructive mining practices had damaged the higher, often drier and more fragile **public lands** of the West. Wildlife and forests vanished in many places. Silt filled watersheds, causing them to dry up. What had been scenic areas now looked like wasted battlefields. John Wesley Powell and John Muir, among others, spoke out for laws to reform the abuses and give-aways of public land. Powerful, resource-dependent industries, such as timber and mining, opposed reform.

National debate and laws passed after 1890 brought forth another revolutionary idea: the people and the land benefit if their government retains some of the remaining public land. Two approaches to managing land influence

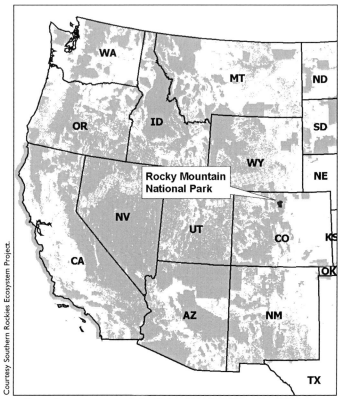

Over ninety percent of the federally-administered public lands, shaded in gray on this map, are located in the western states. All citizens of the United States are owners of the public lands.

the laws—**conservation** and **preservation**. Conservation means managing and consuming resources wisely, as farmers do when they work the land each year while trying to keep it productive for future decades. Preservation involves protecting land in a natural state, with as little human interference as possible.

Enos Mills worked hard for the ideals of conservation and preservation. As snow observer, writer, photographer, and public speaker, he educated people in the practical benefits of conserving natural resources. He also used his talents to preserve many wild places from development.

Today, local, state, and federal public lands make up almost one-third of the area of the United States. Federal government agencies manage the public domain on behalf of its citizen-owners. The U. S. Forest Service, the Fish and Wildlife Service, and the Bureau of Land Management practice both conservation and preservation of natural resources. Preserving parks, cultural and historic sites, and monuments on federal lands is the job of the National Park Service. State and local park agencies preserve additional sites. Using maps and other materials, locate public lands near you and learn about their history and uses.

7 Triumph and Trial
Scenery and Parklands

Each year more than three million visitors flock to Rocky Mountain National Park. They take lots of pictures, have memorable experiences, and spend millions of dollars. But what brings them in the first place? Most are drawn to the park for the scenery.

A century and more ago, conservationists, such as John Muir, Theodore Roosevelt, and Enos Mills, believed that the conservation of scenery was a most important reason for protecting wild lands. People need areas with "eye appeal", they said, for recreation and spiritual refreshment. Many Americans agreed. Efforts to preserve scenic national parks and monuments were often, if not always, successful.

The intuition of the early naturalists was right. Today, through the work of scientists and nature interpreters, people are coming to understand that there is more to scenery than meets the eye. Psychologists believe that children must have contact with nature, through sight and all the senses, to develop into healthy adults. Interpreters share stories that help people know the complex natural processes lying hidden within a scenic vista. Doctors know that hospital patients heal faster in rooms with windows facing natural settings.

Scenery is more than just a pretty face on the landscape. Natural scenery is the looking glass through which we see and begin to understand the essence of life on earth.

A century ago, park booster Enos Mills never anticipated the massive number of visitors who come annually to Rocky Mountain National Park. Some worry that our attraction to the place means "loving the land to death." Overpopulations of people and elk are damaging critical habitats in sections of the preserve. Critics of the National Park Service say the number of people in the park should be limited. Others speak out for the addition of more large predators, such as wolves or human hunters, to reduce wapiti populations. These critics believe that too much use tips the ecological balance away from the resource preservation the park requires.

Even with the park's millions of visitors, **solitude** can be found within the park. Visitors can hike, sleep out, track deer, climb unnamed peaks, spy on a beaver pond, admire a view—all the while meeting few other people. Large portions of the park have no roads or trails. To reduce environmental and social impacts, back country camping permits are limited. No overnight visitors are allowed in the wild southwest corner of the park. Despite numerous problems, Rocky Mountain National Park remains in many ways as scenic and wild as when Enos Mills first explored it. For more information begin your web search at http://www.nps.gov/romo.

Activities for Young Naturalists

The young people of the Trail School, the informal discovery treks Enos Mills fostered at Longs Peak Inn, experienced a mountain world rich in nature's treasures. The activities which follow, adapted from Mills's essay *Children Of My Trail School*, allow modern-day nature explorers to make discoveries in a variety of natural settings, not just mountains. Enos believed that, in any environment, the naturalist's two most powerful tools are interest and imagination.

NATURALIST HIKE
For two or more hikers, ages six to adult.

Mental Tools Needed: Five senses; Curiosity; Interest; Imagination; Recall and retelling.

Equipment Needed: Appropriate clothing; Food; Water; Notebook; Map of the area.

Background: As Enos Mills begins the tale of a naturalist hike, "One summer day nearly twenty years ago a number of boys and girls appeared at my Rocky

Mountain cabin. They wanted me to go with them to the old beaver colony…'It is more than two miles,' I told them, 'and we must walk.' This but added to their desire to go at once. Stepping softly and without saying a word, we slipped through the woods and peeped from behind the last trees into a grassy opening by the beaver pond, hoping for the glimpse of a coyote or deer…." As with Mills and his young naturalists, you never know what new discoveries await until you go in search of them.

Steps to Follow:
1. Locate a natural area which offers opportunity for new discoveries.
2. Explore the area using all the senses it is safe to use. Proceed quietly. Stealth usually provides the best chance for observing wildlife. Avoid getting lost by being aware of the surroundings. Learn to use a compass and maps before you start.
3. Keep track of discoveries in memory or in writing, drawings, photographs, or video.
4. Later, in a classroom, library, or at home, locate more information about the animals, plants and minerals seen. Share findings in writing and illustrations.

NATURE'S STORYBOOK
For two or more observers, ages six to adult.

Mental Tools Needed: Sense of sight; Sense of hearing; Memory; Recall and retelling.

Background: In the words of Enos Mills, "The Trail School methods appear to have developed the constant habit of accurate observation; of learning to see; looking with eager, interested eyes and seeing things as they are. Of an evening when the children are merrily recounting the experiences of the day we are impressed with the fact that they see accurately and recount truthfully, and judge by the evidence." Seeing and retelling accurately are key traits of a good scientist.

Steps to Follow:
1. Sit quietly for a while and observe a natural landscape.
2. Each naturalist points out and briefly describes one or two interesting details seen or heard in the landscape as other group members listen and try to remember them.
3. When landscape descriptions are complete, each person points out and recounts from memory as many of the details shared by others as possible. With larger groups, retelling presents a greater challenge.

Consider breaking into small groups before recounting details.

4. Discuss why powers of observation, memory, and retelling are useful to naturalists.

PERSONAL NATURE TRAILS

For two or a larger group, ages eight to adult.

Mental Tools Needed: Multi-sensory observation and discovery; Memory; Cooperation.

Equipment Needed: Blindfolds for half the group members.

Background: Building a sense of place, a detailed knowledge of an area, requires more than visual skills. Other senses, including sense of direction, are needed to build understanding of a special place.

Steps to Follow:

1. All sit and observe a relatively level natural area, which contains a variety of objects for exploration, such as trees, rocks, lichens, bushes, plant stalks, grasses, or water. The group may want to set an outside boundary for the area of exploration.

2. While making observations, each naturalist selects at least five natural objects he or she wishes to explore up close. Individuals choose a personal nature trail, a route of travel from one object to another and back to the beginning point. Note any potential hazards along the route, such as low branches, rocks that could trip, or holes in the ground.

3. Pair up with a partner. Point out to each other the objects in the order they are to be explored. One partner is blindfolded and sets out to locate the selected natural objects and explore them with every sense, except sight, that it is safe to use. Along the route the sighted partner's job is not to lead, but to give directional clues, if necessary. Keep the blindfolded one safe from harm. Talk as little as possible.

4. After returning to the starting point, partners switch roles.

5. When all complete their explorations, discuss experiences in route-finding and the results of sensory discovery.

6. Individuals may retrace their routes with sight and revisit natural objects up close.

7. Revisit the natural area in other seasons making sensory observations of similarities and differences.

NATIONAL CENSUS

For two or a larger group, ages eight to adult.

Mental Tools Needed: Plant and animal discovery and inventory; Memory; Retelling.

Equipment Needed: Nature field guides and other resource books.

Background: As Enos Mills describes the experience, "We decided to take a census and at once everyone began to count the inhabitants of this (small) nation. We found a number of bugs, spiders, and beetles…and finally everyone surrounded a swarming ant hill, trying to determine how to make an accurate count of this warlike and numerous tribe. This was never settled, for suddenly a big grasshopper with black and yellow wings entered the nation from the outside. He alighted for only a moment and then flew away again. The opinion was equally divided as whether he should be counted as one of the inhabitants or an invader."

Steps to Follow:

1. Locate a site with numerous plant, insect, and even reptile or mammal residents. An area near a stream or

an overgrown field border works well. A mowed blue-grass lawn might not.

2. Each naturalist measures off a nation, a roughly-square area five giant steps per side. Mark corners (national boundaries) with rocks or sticks. Make a quick population inventory of insects, animals, and plants for this new nation. Share any special curiosities found with the group. At this point, being able to name the creatures found is less important than making discoveries.

3. When censuses are complete, share the results from memory and try to answer any questions raised by the discoveries. Leave any discoveries where they were found.

4. Later, in a classroom, library, or at home, locate more information about the inhabitants of the nation and share findings in writing and illustrations.

FOR FURTHER STUDY
Visit Enos Mills Cabin Museum
6760 Colorado Highway 7
Estes Park, CO 80517-6404
970-586-4706
enosmillscbn@earthlink.net
http://home.earthlink.net/~enosmillscbn/

Timeline

1870 – Enos Abijah Mills, Jr. born on April 22 in Linn County, Kansas.

1884 – Travels to Estes Park, Colorado. Works at Elkhorn Lodge for the summer.

1885 – Works at Longs Peak House. Climbs Longs Peak for first time. Begins to build homestead cabin.

1886 – Works summer at Longs Peak House, helping guide climbers and build Longs Peak Trail. Finishes homestead cabin.

1887 – Makes first solo climb of Longs Peak. Treks to Butte, Montana in fall to work in copper mines. Continues mining during winters in Montana and Colorado, off and on until 1902.

1889 – Guides first Longs Peak climbing party. Travels to California. Meets John Muir.

1890 – Visits wild lands throughout California for six months. Takes business courses in fall.

1891 – Explores Yellowstone region in spring; works the summer for a U. S. government surveying crew.

1892 – Treks glaciers and coastal mountains in southeast Alaska, and again in 1894.

1890-1900 – Travels extensively in wild lands and rivers of western North America. Guides most summers in Estes Park.

1895 – Makes his first speech on forests in Kansas City.

1900 – Sails to Europe for month-long tour with Elkanah Lamb.

1902 – Buys Longs Peak House from Carlyle Lamb. Publishes first article in a national magazine.

1902-1905 – Makes numerous high-mountain winter expeditions as Colorado Snow Observer.

1905 – Self-publishes first book, *The Story of Estes Park and a Guide Book*. Begins first national speaking tour in fall.

1906 – Longs Peak Inn burns. Designs and oversees rebuilding of larger inn. Completes last season as Longs Peak guide.

1907-1909 – Tours nation as Government Lecturer on Forestry, appointed by President Roosevelt.

1909 – *Wild Life on the Rockies* published, with 14 more books to follow. Begins national park campaign for Estes Park region.

1915 – Rocky Mountain National Park created by act of Congress.

1916 – Campaigns for and helps plan the creation of the National Park Service, which occurs in August.

1918 – Marries Esther Burnell. Speaks against concessions in national parks.

1919 – Daughter Enda born April 27.

1922 – Dies at home on September 22.

Glossary

abolitionist – a person who supports abolishing the practice of slavery

Bleeding Kansas – a name given to eastern Kansas Territory after 1854, describing its bloody battles over the issue of slavery

brood – the young of animals, especially birds, raised at the same time

chaperonage – an older person watching over children on a field trip

communities – all of the plants and animals in a certain area interacting to create a distinct type of environment (also called **ecosystems, ecological communities,** and **communities of life**). In the Great Plains and southern Rocky Mountains, some of the communities include:

prairie or **grassland**, communities usually lying below 6,000-7,000 feet in elevation, whose dominant species are grasses and the animals who depend on grasses; the **montane** zone, a mountain region of forest and meadow extending from about 8,000 to 9,500 feet in elevation;

the **subalpine** zone, a mountain community of dense forests, meadows, and wetlands, stretching from about 9,500 to 11,500 feet in elevation;

the **alpine** zone, a mountain region of low-growing shrubs, grasses, and other flowering plants, which reaches from tree limit at about 11,500 feet to above 14,000 feet in elevation

conservation – managing and consuming natural resources wisely

conservationist – a person who works to keep natural resources, such as forests and clean water, from being used up, so that future generations may also share in the resources

concessions – companies that provide services to visitors in national parks and other public facilities, under contract with the managing agency of the facility

consumptive – a person suffering from consumption, also known as tuberculosis, a disease of the lungs

dust devil – a swirling mass of wind-driven dirt and debris, often seen sweeping across the prairie or other dry places like a miniature tornado (also called a **whirlwind**)

greenhorn – an inexperienced newcomer to an area; a term derived from the green or immature horns of a young animal

homestead – public land occupied and improved by a settler under the conditions of the U.S. Homestead Act

homestead patent – the ownership title to a piece of land, transferring it from the U. S. government to a private owner

lecture tour – a series of speeches given by the same lecturer in several locations

milling – crushing a mined ore to make it ready for smelting

naturalist – a person knowledgeable about plants, animals, weather and geology, who enjoys exploring and observing the natural world

nature guiding – an occupation, partly originated by Enos Mills, that encourages visitors to natural areas to learn about the environment (also called **nature interpreter**)

park – an open, often grassy valley surrounded by mountains

preservation – protecting land in a natural state, with as little human interference as possible

public land – land owned by all of the people of a nation or region and administered on their behalf by a land management agency, such as a park service, forest service, or park and recreation department

public land disposal – selling, trading, or giving away public land, so that it becomes private land

smelting – to obtain a metal from an ore by heating and melting it, usually in a furnace

solitude – being alone, often in an out-of-the-way place, such as in a forest or near an ocean

tree limit – the place where cold, wind, snow depth, frozen soil, and other elements stop tree growth. Beyond tree limit the alpine zone begins

tundra – the name given to the low-growing shrubs, grasses, and other flowering plants that cling to the often-rocky soils of the alpine community of life

wise use – consuming natural resources in a way that retains some for future use

Bibliography

WORKS BY ENOS MILLS

Mills, Enos A. *Adventures of a Nature Guide and Essays in Interpretation.* Estes Park, CO: Temporal Mechanical Press, 2001 (1920).

_____. *Being Good To Bears and Other Animal 'Tails'.* Estes Park, CO: Temporal Mechanical Press, 1999 (1919 and 1930).

_____. *Bird Memories of the Rockies.* Estes Park, CO: Temporal Mechanical Press, 2000 (1931).

_____. *The Story of Early Estes Park, Rocky Mountain National Park, and Grand Lake.* Estes Park, CO: Temporal Mechanical Press, 1999 (1905).

_____. *The Grizzly, Our Greatest Wild Animal.* Sausalito, CA: Comstock Editions, 1973 (1919) and Estes Park, CO: Temporal Mechanical Press, 1999 .

_____. *In Beaver World.* Estes Park, CO: Temporal Mechanical Press, 2001 (1913).

_____. *Rocky Mountain National Park.* Estes Park, CO: Temporal Mechanical Press, 2001 (1924).

_____. *The Rocky Mountain Wonderland.* Estes Park, CO: Temporal Mechanical Press, 2002   (1915).

_____. *Romance of Geology.* Estes Park, CO: Temporal Mechanical Press, 2000 (1926).

_____. *The Spell of the Rockies.* Estes Park, CO: Temporal Mechanical Press, 2004 (1911).

_____. *The Story of a Thousand Year Pine.* Estes Park, CO: Temporal Mechanical Press, 1999 (1914).

_____. *Stories of Scotch.* Estes Park, CO: Temporal Mechanical Press, 2000 (1916).

_____. *Waiting in the Wilderness.* Estes Park, CO: Temporal Mechanical Press, 2000 (1921).

_____. *Watched by Wild Animals*. Estes Park, CO: Temporal Mechanical Press, 2000 (1922)

_____. *Wild Animal Homesteads*. Estes Park, CO: Temporal Mechanical Press, 2000 (1923)

_____. *Wild Life on the Rockies*. Estes Park, CO: Temporal Mechanical Press, 2004 (1909)

_____. *Your National Parks*. Estes Park, CO: Temporal Mechanical Press, 2002 (1917).

SOURCES

Buckholz, C.W. *Rocky Mountain National Park: A History*. Boulder, CO: Colorado Associated University Press, 1983.

Hawthorne, Hildegarde and Esther Burnell Mills. *Enos Mills of the Rockies*. Estes Park, CO: Temporal Mechanical Press, 2001 (1935).

Drummond, Alexander. *Enos Mills: Citizen of Nature*. Niwot, CO: University Press of Colorado, 1995.

RELATED PUBLICATIONS

Barron, T. A. *High as a Hawk: A Brave Girl's Historic Climb*. Illustrated by Ted Lewin. New York: Philomel Books, 2004.

Fielder, John, T. A. Barron, and Enos Mills. *Rocky Mountain National Park: A 100 Year Perspective*. Photographs by John Fielder and Enos Mills. Englewood, CO: Westcliffe Publishers, 1995.

Index

Acknowledgments

Writing a biography focused on one person requires the contributions of many. Among those concerned with the life and works of Enos Mills, I especially want to recognize: The Colorado Endowment for the Humanities, Denver, Colorado, for providing a grant to support research on this project. Alexander Drummond, for extensive and invaluable background information and for text review. The staff of the Denver Public Library Western History Department, the location of the Enos Mills Collection. The staff of the Colorado Historical Society Hart Library for research assistance. Ola May Earnest, Linn County Historical and Genealogical Society, Pleasanton, Kansas, for guidance in research on the Mills and Lamb families. The staff of the Rocky Mountain National Park library for photo research assistance. Enda Mills Kiley, for direction in exploring her father's life. The Mills-Kiley family, for their perpetuation of numerous elements in the legacy of Enos Mills. T. A. Barron and John Fielder, for understanding the importance of wild places and the contributions of Enos Mills to wilderness preservation. Connor Bailey, Southern Rockies Ecosystem Project, for map preparation. Rick and Michelle Eckert, for companionship on the trail and help with digital photography. Carol Wood Stansfield, for continual support and for nurturing a new generation of naturalists at the School in the Woods.

About the Author

Storyteller and author John Stansfield began exploring western North America as a boy in 1960 and has never stopped. He loves hiking and skiing the West and telling stories about its diverse lands, wildlife, and people. He presents a one-man show for all ages reenacting the life of Enos Mills. Stansfield is the author of *John Denver: Man of the World* (Filter Press, 2008) and *Writers of the American West: Multicultural Learning Encounters* (Teacher Ideas Press, 2002), which earned a Colorado Authors' League Award and was a finalist for the Colorado Book Award. He received an Oracle Award from National Storytelling Network in 2008.

John works to protect Colorado's wild places. For these efforts, the Wilderness Society presented him an Environmental Heroes Award in 2004. He and his wife, Carol, live in Larkspur, Colorado, on the high divide between the South Platte and Arkansas Rivers within view of Longs Peak.

Contact John at jorcstan@juno.com

More
Now You Know Bios

Susan Anderson: Colorado's Doc Susie
by Lydia Griffin
Beginning in 1909, Doc Susie practiced medicine in Grand
County for more than forty years.
ISBN: 978-0-86541-108-1 pb $8.95

Unsinkable: The Molly Brown Story
by Joyce B. Lohse
Heroine of the Titanic disaster and philanthropist.
ISBN: 978-0-86541-081-7 pb $8.95

Chipeta: Ute Peacemaker
by Cynthia S. Becker
Ute peacemaker and wife of Chief Ouray.
ISBN: 978-086541-091-6 pb $8.95

Frank Craig: Medical Visionary
by Herb Tabak
Established a Denver tent colony in 1907 for indigent victims of
tuberculosis. Craig Hospital is named for him.
ISBN: 978-0-86541-127-2 pb $8.95

John Denver: Man for the World
by John Stansfield
Popular singer, songwriter, and humanitarian. He wrote "Rocky
Mountain High", one of Colorado's two state songs.
ISBN: 978-086541-088-6 pb $8.95

Justina Ford: Medical Pioneer
by Joyce B. Lohse
First African-American woman to practice medicine in Colorado.
ISBN: 978-0-86541-074-9 pb $8.95

Jose Dario Gallegos: Merchant of the Santa Fe Trail
by Emerita Romero-Anderson
Established the first store in San Luis, the oldest town in Colorado.
ISBN: 978-0-86541-084-8 pb $8.95

Emily Griffith: Opportunity's Teacher
by Joyce B. Lohse
Educator who founded Denver's Emily Griffith Technical
College in 1916.
ISBN: 978-0-86541-077-0 pb $8.95

Dottie Lamm: A Friend to Families
by Emily B. Warner
Journalist, social activist, and former first lady of Colorado.
ISBN: 978-086541-085-5 pb $8.95

Mary Elitch Long: First Lady of Fun
by Debra B. Faulkner
Founder of Elitch Gardens zoo and amusement park.
ISBN: 978-086541-094-7 pb $8.95

Martha Maxwell: Natural History Pioneer
by James McVey
Naturalist, innovative taxidermist, and museum founder.
ISBN: 978-0-86541-075-6 pb $8.95

General William Palmer: Railroad Pioneer
by Joyce B. Lohse
Civil War hero and railroad pioneer who founded
Colorado Springs.
ISBN: 978-0-86541-092-3   pb $8.95

John Wesley Powell: Soldier, Explorer, Scientist
by Jean Thor Cook
Civil War hero who led the first exploration of the Grand Canyon.
ISBN: 978-0-86541-080-0   pb $8.95

Florence Sabin: Teacher, Scientist, Humanitarian
by E. E. Duncan
First woman to be elected to the National Academy of Sciences,
she led an overhaul of Colorado public health laws.
ISBN: 978-0-86541-139-5   pb $8.95

Bob Sakata: American Farmer
by Daniel Blegen
Interned at Topaz Relocation Center in Utah during World
War II, Sakata established the highly successful Sakata
Farms near Brighton.
ISBN: 978-086541-093-0   pb $8.95

Edward Wynkoop: Soldier and Indian Agent
by Nancy Oswald
A founder of Denver and outspoken critic of the Sand
Creek Massacre.
ISBN: 978-0-86541-184-5   pb $8.95